Truth Serum
Watering Seasons of My Love
A Poetry Collection

Autumn Reign

Published By:
Belfrey Books

Copyright © 2012 by Nicole Randolph

all rights reserved,

No part of this publication may be reproduced, distributed, or transmitted in any form or by any means, without the prior written permission of the publisher, except in the case of brief quotations embodied in critical reviews and certain other noncommercial uses permitted by copyright law.

First Belfrey Books Edition 2012

For information address:

BELFREY BOOKS

275 East 4th Street Suite 400
Saint Paul, MN 55101

Printed in the United States of America

Publisher's Cataloging-in-Publication data
Reign, Autumn
Truth Serum: Watering Seasons of My Love, A Poetry Collection
p. cm.

ISBN 978-0-983 6504-1-6

1. Poetry 2. Relationships 3. Love

Acknowledgements

IN LOVING MEMORY
For Trudy "Matuka" Fernandez and Jerry "Vito" Diggs my parents, I am grateful for their unapologetic honesty, infectious spirits and passion for life. It is with great pleasure to know that I was conceived out of a beautiful union of love. It is out of this love that I have had a lifelong desire to learn the depth of love. It is from my inception that I have been in love with and in pursuit of the penetrating essence of love. For it is what I am truly made of ...love.

A NOTE OF THANKS
Thank you to my sister, Michelle for editing and Christine and Nathan for helping make my dream come true.

This book is dedicated with love to:

The greatest gifts god has given me are my talents and children and for that I am truly thankful.

The greatest loves of my life are Jazzmin Briahna, Justice Ja'Vonne, and Malcolm Marsailis.

I have had many dreams of having the perfect love, but it does not get any better than motherhood.

Their love is veracious and sincere. I want my children to have many dreams, dream often and never give up on their dreams. I pray they will love them enough to make them come true!

Foreword

A young scientist draped in her crisp white medical garb, peered over the top of her burgundy rectangle specs. Her mind tingled with various notions of why the phenomenon in front of her just occurred. A white lab rat was offered the opportunity to enjoy a tasty treat all to himself. But just a few dozen rat steps away, another furry lab rat sat helplessly trapped in a cage. She was pleading for freedom and food in sounds that could be endearing to only her own kind.

To the young scientist's surprise, the free rat hurried over to the cage. With his tiny pink paws, he pressed a conspicuous lever which released the trapped rat. They then scurried over to the tasty treat and enjoyed it together in harmony. I read about this experiment in a neurology journal. Scientist postulated several causes for the rat's behavior. Yet, as scientist often do, they overlooked the intangible cause, which is where the truth often lies.

The cause they overlooked is the eternal element that unites all creation. It is deep complexity that makes the element arcane. But Autumn Reign's collection of poems creates a vivid multi-dimensional painting that burst forth with an unimaginable array of hues. Her composition of words makes the intangible, tangible.

Through silky metaphors and fiery frankness, these poems explore all the realms that lie both on the surface and in the dark abyss of this living element. It is the essence of the human endeavor and the reason why life excels. It is the reason why even a despicable lowly life form such as a rat, chose to emancipate another rodent and share his meal with her. This life unifying eternal element is L-O-V-E.

Prepare your soul for an awakening inoculation. Autumn Reign shares her experiences and observations of love through poems that shed light on a mystery that entangles us all.

From intimate heartbreak to motherly love, from self-love to community love, Autumn Reign's poems are potent enough to pierce the impenetrable heart of a hardened prisoner serving a life sentence such as myself. So I am certain that you will also be touched and awakened by the infectious TRUTH SERUM.

Jeffery Young #213390
Minnesota Department of Corrections Prisoner
Educator
Minnesota Spokesman Recorder Columnist

Contents

Acknowledgements   3

Foreword   7

Introduction   15

Section One   17
  Love

    In Love   19
    Waiting On You   20
    Her Window   21
    Have You Ever Loved Like This?   22
    Love's Gift   23
    Just A Little Bit   24
    Lie Down Love   25
    The Love I Crave   26
    Our Time Together   27
    My Prayer For Your Love   28
    Love Regardless   29
    Water Love   31
    I Never Meant To   33

Section Two   35
  Spells

    Lovers   37
    Jones Love   38
    Tenderness   39

Loving You	41
A Poem For You	42
My Haiku For You	43
L.S.D.	44
Music Made In The Afternoon	45
The Sun Kissing Me	46
Cotton Candy Skies	47
My Light	48
Good Hands Tonight	50

Section Three 51
Vicissitudes

Whenever The Wind Blows (WTWB)	53
A Timeless Love Reigns Supreme	55
Soft & Sexy	56
My Heart	57
I Have Had	58
She Did It With A Flash	59
R.E.S.P.E.C.T.	60
For The Sir In My Life	61
When Daddy Left	63
My Pocket	64
They Pump Me Up	65

Section Four 67
Reverberations (Echos)

The Best Gift	69
Birthed	71
No Invitation Needed	72
Righteous Anger	74
Why She Hurts	76

Dear Lover	77
When Love Calls	78
Autumn's Blues	79
Just Call Me Mysty	82
Broken Wing	83
Speak To Me	84
Windows Pain	85
Mirrored Image	86

Section Five 87
New Lenses

No Thank You	89
It's Pouring	90
She Looks Like A Lady	91
With A Thankful Heart	92
You'll Learn My Name	93
Tempting temptations	95
If	96
If (II)	97
Fortress In A Dress	99
Autumn's Spring	101
A Poem For The Wounded	102
I Offer You	103
Reflection	104
Rebirth	105
Sweet Peace	106
Sister Without A Name	107
Walking Across My Mind	109
Again You Walked	110

Section Six
Truth Serum
111

Truth Serum, The Truth About Lies	113
Ain't That A Bitch…	114
Visits	115
When I Reflect	116
For The Love Of Tea	117
Your Box	118
Autumn's Fall	119
Kissing Me	120
Can You Forgive Me	121
Our Daily Bread	122
Not Kindness Or Weakness	124
You Won't Make Me Over But He Will	126
Stormy Monday	127
Changing Lanes	128
He's No Cupcake	129
I Guess You Did Not Know	131
You Loving Me	133
Call Me Elsa	135

Section Seven
Black Roses
137

Pretty Brown Penny	139
Daddy	141
No Room In The In	142
Black Rose	144
The Black Man's Hands	145
America In Black	147

Heartbreaker	148
Dark Angel	151
He's An Angel	152
I Am Not A Story Teller	153
Daddy's Ray's	154

Section Eight   155
Family

Where Love Is Concerned	157
Natural Flowing Hair	158
Race Car	159
Music	160
Ode To Ma'ter	161
My Dope Fiend Father	162
My Soul Is On Fire	163

Section Nine   167
Soul Collection

Quotes	169

Afterword   173

Introduction

It is in somber moments that I have wrestled with this pursuit of love. Looking, seeking, living and dying while loving. There have been moments that I have shared boundless ecstasy and great pain. In short momentary lapses, I found myself repeating this journey once more. This time, I was smarter and stronger only to find myself weakened like kryptonite. I am melting not from boiling water but from the pleasure of another love affair. As time lapsed, I would succumb to the depth of despair when love lost it fierce fiery flame.

The douses of nature's midst moving through my love and life have been swift, but never without warnings of the coming of the dawn. These loves have been some of the most beautiful blues, deep mahoganies and some with cotton candy skies. These beckoning of experiences have helped me create my life's best work. It is through these loves, I found that I am a lover and a friend who wants to allow my mate a rare opportunity.

It is my hope that he will experience the sweet simplicity of love. This brutal honesty of self is yet offered to many and the truth serum many refuse to swallow. I ask if you will drink with me, a little sip and taste words of my love's hopes, with its peaks, valleys and hidden sunsets. I invite you to partake and when you are done, make your love more honest and unapologetic. I dare you to risk loving like you have never loved before. You could not imagine the rapture. I dare you to love like it is your last time to love.

Section One

LOVE

Journey,
Beauty
and Bliss

In Love

I can admit it

Yes, I am in love with love

Yes I walk as though I have air floating under my feet

I can smile at passersby and wink at an old man and a little boy too for that matter

I am in love with love and I find beauty in everything I see, especially when I see you

Love lives here, resides here and on a regular basis, love plays here, love lays here, love sings here, love dances here, love takes long walks just to admire the trees, love sees beauty, there's love even in the leaves

I can admit it, yes I am in love with love and yes I do walk as if I have waterfalls flowing from my feet, for love takes me on journey's I have never dreamed, what's most beautiful is I would have never known this kind of love if it were not for you

Because you ooze love, because you drip love unafraid to share your love of the journey to one's heart, you make a cold rainy day seem like it is 90 degrees and sunny, I am in love with love because you have taught me how to love at will and you decided to hold my heart first even before you choose to love me.

Yes, I am in love with love because he taught me how

WAITING ON YOU

I saw you today

You sauntered right by my window acting as if I were not staring right at you

welcoming you into my life offering you all the best I had to give.

I know you do not come around often, you're hard to hold on to and I am even lucky that you stopped by at all

But I want you to know that I have been working hard, to give myself

You

Recognizing how important it is to see you in my own face, lips, hips and thighs recognizing that with you there are no limits to where we can go, I have learned to give you and receive you, now you will truly understand

I am in love with you

LOVE (smile)

Her Window

As you open the window to (ME)

I pray that you like what you see

And grow to love all that I have to offer

I have rainbows to share with ribbons

As we flow, glide and soar

We will create a bond between souls

Minds meeting yours and yours meeting mine

Preparation, introductions and near collisions at times with recovery and discovery

We will take trips on unpaved roads

What I want to be is your landing gear in my air field whenever you need to come in for an emergency landing or simply when you just need to come home

I want to be able to greet you with so much love dripping from my arms and I will be so full of pleasures and treasures for you that I can supply your every need at your every whim, because I love you

One day, someday I hope to open the window to my heart and let you make your landing within

Have you ever loved like this?

Although I may not have always told you

What was in my head or heart?

The love may have been absent in words

But present in the kiss

Or in the long still look

I have thoroughly enjoyed

Just holding your hand

Knowing that I am with you

My love has not been thunderous

But it has been calm satisfying moments

when I have Loved you

ONLY...

Love's Gift

Love's gifts are special

It can't be your needs and wants

True gifts for your love

Just a Little Bit

Oh, Love why do I try so hard to grasp you when I know you are beyond my reach and each time we meet I am scared with fresh tears that I have cried for you and newly revealed wounds

Love let me in or let me go

Spare me the unnecessary battles to no avail

Why are you so important to me

I know I am human, but love

I have been told your love is not kind to anyone so each time I try I still end up with bits and pieces of this thing called love never making my life whole or complete

Love still escapes me

Even in my dreams

Lie Down Love

I want to lie you down on my lap

with your chest resting on my thighs

your head and shoulders leaning on pillows

on high

I will gently rub your shoulders until your body goes limp

surrender for it is only me

let go release your thoughts

for a moment of pleasure

I will tell you what you mean to me

and why I am glad I am here for you

with each stroke up and down your

spine to your neck then your temples

rotating in a circular motion

I am here for you, just relax and let it flow

I am going to be gentle and I promise not to stop

I want you to turn over but before

I massage your chest; I slowly lean toward you and kiss you sweetly on your lips

The Love I Crave

The love I want, the love I crave is gentle and warm:

it is sincere and true, soft and kind

it is forgiving and humble, sensitive and real

it is passionate and withstanding, safe and secure

it is fulfilling and complete, intense and purposeful

it has meaning and depth, is constant and satisfying it soothes the soul and spirit, it is spontaneous and inquisitive

it is a continuous discovery, patient and careful

it is not selfish, but tenacious and honest, perhaps it has direction, versatile and freaky, it won't let go, wholesome and vocal, and it speaks of honesty

The love I want, the love I crave is active and alive and with each day the thoughts brings me more happiness

Perhaps someday I will receive the love I want and THE LOVE I CRAVE!

Our Time Together

For Arts Sake,

We peeled back our eyelids to reveal windowpanes of our souls

Unrehearsed songs of our solemn

Melodies of our origin

Laced with lyrics of our future selves

The tempo for opportunities to jam once more

The beauty was the acceptance

While viewing rare masterpieces of art at first glance

Time well spent for the sake of the true artist.

(ONESELF)

MY PRAYER FOR YOUR LOVE

(On your wedding day)

My prayer for you as one body is that GOD continues to fill your hearts with an abundance of love and kindness for one another that will last all the days of your lives

May you never feel the cold of the world but always be sheltered by the warmth of GOD's Love and your love for each other

By his words only will you stand and live fruitfully and when others fall and cease I pray that your faith will make you unmovable and steadfast with purpose, patience and understanding

As you grow in serving the Lord, I wish you God's speed with each day that passes by

May you remember to put God first in all that you do as you join hands in God's Love and begin your life together

I pray that now you abide by faith, hope and love and of these three, I pray for the True Blessings of Love

LOVE REGARDLESS

Only the strong survive, you're smart and strong, that's what they say

And I thought

No I am not strong; I just learned how to suffer through the pain

I learned how to accept my short comings and those of others who could not give me the love I needed

Sure many men say they take it, some women say they fake it, but just the same it is a lie

See, I would rather love and feel love and be loved like the music in a love song

Can I get an Amen for, Teach me how, Take me away, first and foremost, Turn me on

But until that day comes I am going to have to settle for what my mind musters up each day, like when I see a couple bursting with smiles just because they are able to hold a glimpse of each other in their eye

Then I find myself savoring moments in movies that, portray love lost and rekindled, supreme loves over time and love that won't love anyone else because like those lovelies, I have a little romantic in my back pocket and a snippet in my purse

See many women are afraid to let you know love lies deep within and it takes a serious heavy duty construction worker type that has warm marshmallows of moments in his front pants pocket with gentle hands that know how to grip

And men are really ready at different times, than women but when he says he loves you it is from the top of his head to the soles of your feet, he then needs a waist of warmth and lap of kindness and loyalty that soothes him when nothing else does

I know he exist because there have been times in my life when I have kissed him whenever the wind blew and he would stroke my hand with his and then we too walked off into someone else's sunset of love.

This may have sounded like an confusing poem about the lapse of loving moments in one's life, but what it is saying is that there is love all around us and within us

If we would just let ourselves free to feel the sweetness of another's caress and be willing to get naked with ourselves and share what is beneath the tips of our breast and the helms of our thighs and at the nape of his neck and in the arch of his back, can we love the innermost part of one another, then only can we

Set our wings free and glide into the tenderness of love

WATER LOVE

Can you hear the water?

Can you feel the water?

Can you see the water flowing?

Can you feel the force of my nature's call for you?

Please hear my cry

Do you know what I need, Do you know what I am asking for?

You should know simply because you say you love

Loving me starts with my soul, spirit, inner self, the her inside of me

Comfort her, talk with her if you dare, she may even tell you things I would not

Spend some time to get to know her, if you cannot reach her you have lost me already!

Do you come to play never intending to stay, Can you hear the water flowing inside of me

Take a sip of my sweetness it will set off a numbing tranquil mood that will soothe your mind body and soul, I will talk to you in ways and languages you've never known

I will touch you just as the wind does when it blows gently, with subtle touches exploring you everywhere

Awakening places within yourself that you did not know existed

You will begin to speak and sing sweet sorrow for you never knew it could be so good, you never knew you were missing me all this time

Calling the water in you, just as I run to it, always,

Can you hear the water?

Can you see the water flowing within my spirit?

Take a moment to bathe yourself in a river of love, a sea of truth, in an ocean of faith

Bathe yourself in my everlasting rhythm

For the rewards are deeper, even

Can you hear the water?

I do…

We talk everyday…

I NEVER MEANT TO

As I fell up my stairs

I realized I loved you

I fell on the bed

Blushing

Wrapping myself with

Thoughts of you

I jumped in the shower

With splashes of water

Brought me flashes of you

It made me cover my mouth

As I skipped into my room

All while twirling my curly Afro

I kiss at myself in the mirror

And I lick my lips

As I apply my lipstick

I hug myself

For

I know I love you

I never meant to

But

I know

I love you

Section Two

Spells

Bittersweet
Moments of
Splendor

LOVERS

Love, whip cream, cherries, champagne, satin sheets, sweat, wetness, hours, a.m., men women, rhythm, beats, drums, sounds of the midnight hour

Voices of song, music, melody, happiness, carefree, careful, feelings, evolution, deeper, cheaper, less than the cost of buying a cow why do that when you can have 2%

Late night drives, early morning cries of passion, quenching your thirst, drinking from the fountain of my soul, bearer of it all, loving you day and night, that's what I do rubbing your back

Baking sweets mainly me, following your lead, spending more than my time on you is what I do, Pillow talk, breakfast our long good bye's only to say hello in the a.m. when we wake

Let go, go away, time to leave it's over, the ride is over, nothing to show but the dried up dead roses you once gave me when I was blue

What I didn't know was the sadness began with you, some lovers know where to begin and when to end, now you are gone, we were just lovers nothing more, the next time I will ask for your resume up front!

Jones Love

I got a jones love, I got love on my mind

I got a jones love at least one, two or three times a day

It makes me, wakes me and takes me to places I have never known, positions and procession a true art form

I got a jones for this man and it may not be love but what I do know, it calls my name so sweetly let me tell you the pied piper has nothing on him

Just kicking it is what we say, spending time enjoying each other and we do the do and other thangs

I got a serious love jones for this man and he knows the game, but what I don't understand is how this all came to be, I have been told when the love jones comes down on ya!

It is nothing short of destiny, so Mr. Love Jones, from the top of my head to the bottom of my feet, let's continue playing this song, for the last verse will be bitter sweet sorrow with honey dew, I will be missing my Mr. Love Jones

I will miss Jones'in with you!

Tenderness

Weekend of tenderness

Gently probing

Sweetness dripping

Gliding fingernails

Sending syrupy sensations

Welcoming caresses

Flavored hands

To your domain

Tempt me

I will answer

Taming your soul

Realms of your desire

Faint palpitations

Afflict me

Bake sweetness

Awaken feelings

Remembering

A little tenderness

When it

Felt so damn

Good

Loving you

Loving u has always been cloudy on a clear day. I can feel the warmth inside but it escapes my grasp. I can see the gentleness and feel its caresses, but it eludes me. I run towards you but when you catch me, you hold me until I slip through your fingers.

And no matter how many times the wind blows, my kisses land on your cheek, and you did not notice I have been there all the time. Waiting and wondering if you would ever call for me again, would you need me as much as I have always needed you.

Loving me, I know has not been easy, especially when my life has been consumed by thunderstorms of life. No matter the threat of thunder in the sky, you have been the lightening that has illuminated my heart, I cannot always express why or when, but the light has always been there shining waiting for your return.

Loving you has always been cloudy on a clear day.

A Poem for You

There's a poem for every life situation

There's a poem for your blues and your wrongs

And for your let's get it on's

There's a poem for your good times and bad

And for the moments when you are feeling sad

There's a poem for the morning dew when I am lying with you

And for your rain and your rainbows too

There's a poem for every reason and each season

There's a poem for the tiniest loves which is sweetest of them all.

My haiku for you

When I kiss your lips

Warmth fills my body's edges

Kissing you sugary sweet

L.S.D.

My thighs sing

Verses to your drum

The rhythms call to you

Closer

Stronger

Longing to be within

Your grasps

I safely

Close my eyes

Lay my head

For I am with you

Love

Long Sweet Delectables

Lingering Savory Delights

Long Slow Doses

Lucid Sultry Dates

My thighs sung

Music made in the afternoon

I miss Blu's music, the lyrics use to dance up and down my spine while the notes and cords of his guitar sent unidentifiable rhythms to my inner most core, arranging the chambers of my orchestra creating melodious symphonies that my body never heard

Each time he moved to and fro, my sweet sanctum was beckoned from and to Then all of a sudden our lips met at the place we were last denied, but this time my flute played a soft key that he not only remembered

He missed running his fingers up and down the slopes of my arching back and the curves of my vanilla hips, he stroked my moist grooves grasping tighter each time so tightly that I could not resist any more

I chose to let our harmonies, syncopate as we drew closer and closer to our sweet song of yesterday all while we enjoyed the pleasing music of our afternoon delight…

The Sun Kissing Me

The sun kisses my skin on Tuesday morning

Not harshly but bitter sweetly it taste the vanilla in my hue

Before you know it I am as golden as you

Sweetly the sun kisses me from head to toe

It savors my skin even as the wind blows

Gently it covers me with a blanket, a glove

The sun feels so good it must be love

Cotton Candy Skies

I am in awe at the scribe in the sky

The creations of color pleasing to the eyes

Sketches of pinks, blues and purples

Dance across the sky

I smile at the Cotton Candy

The sweetness cradles me while

I witness the beauty

I am thankful for gods

Cotton Candy Skies

My light

She is my light, my joy

My Ebony Princess

She is the brightest of sun rays in a world of darkness

She dances streams of light and lays on the crescent moon, light beams all around her

She is my daughter, she is love

She is my light, my peace

My Sugar Princess

She illuminates a room with her smile, she is honey sweet

She engulfs others with her tranquil mothering senses

She paints tapestries of beauty and color abounds with each stroke

She is my daughter, she is love

He is my light, my heart

My Ebony Prince

He is gentle in spirit and strong in will

He has boundless energy as he seeks to compete and win

He takes pleasure in helping those in need

He is my son, he is love

My children are my light and my heart

Good hands tonight

I need you more than I ever have in my life and what I need from you is nothing extra ordinary, it is to just ask

May we hold hands tonight?

All I need is to simply hold your hand

I will still nestle myself in your chest, just like I always do to feel safe and secure, I have the desire to be close to you, I want you as my blanket from the world tonight, no more interaction is required

All I need is to simply hold your hand

As I am lying close to you, I will listen to your heart beat and then mine, just to see if we truly have the rhythm in our hearts to make this long journey

All I need is to simply hold your hand

I want to listen to you speak to me gently, softly and sweetly in your baritone voice and I will listen intently as I draw nearer to you as we become one, the comfort zone I seek is made as I simply hold your hand as you hold me

I came home from work tonight needing your love, to welcome me in from the cold, and it was not a hug or a kiss, I needed from you, it was to simply hold your hand, the comfort zone I seek is made as I hold your hand as you hold me

All I need is to simply hold your hand

May we just hold hands tonight?

Section Three

VICISSITUDES

Ebbing
and
Flowing

WHENEVER THE WIND BLOWS (WTWB)

As I leave you this winter

Please remember these words

And think of me!

WHENEVER THE WIND BLOWS

I will be kissing you

Whenever you feel alone

My arms will hold you tight

Whenever you are tired or weary

I will be your strength

Whenever you feel pain

I will wash it all away

Whenever you feel incomplete

I will make you whole

Whenever you are in doubt

I will have faith in you

Whenever you are in need

I will be there

Always remember

WHENEVER THE WIND BLOWS

I will be kissing you…

A TIMELESS LOVE REIGNS SUPREME

The love of my life is my lover for life; for he knew me when I did not know myself, when others watched me he studied me

The love of my life knows my word selection and heard my thoughts

He was there to hold me while I spoke, he listened to my words but he heard my heart

The love of my life offers tranquil moments of love while he sits quietly with his lover for life by the ocean's shore

The love of my life is my lover for life even though we have never loved at all, time and distance cannot erase was lies deep within us

When I hold him I hold his heart in my hands as his head is placed gently in my lap, I listen to his words that are so soft they sound like sweet murmurs

My lover for life is the love of my life; he is my gentle giant, honest and loving, I knew him when he didn't know that I would love him for life, our love would never die, it would be eternal as the flame burning inside my heart, he's my lover for life.

Our love reigns supreme.

Soft & Sexy

I want to bring soft and sexy back to a time where loving is sweet and sultry morning dew all of these are reminisce of loving you

The arch in my back and slope of my nose are the secret places of the melody of our music making

It is long and tasty with a sundry of pleasure with supplications of your sculpted body

How incredible is your love and presence pours raindrops on my mane and droplets in crevices of my hidden places,

You bring me to your gentle clasps and I welcome your lips and positions of our love

You bring the soft and I bring the sexy back to our love…

My heart

My heart lies beneath the earth where it is dark.

Where the earth speaks, and opens cracks of my soul, leaking glimpses of my innermost being where my passions lie.

My heart is kept in a sacred place out of the eyes view and the hands caress.

My heart lies beneath the earth where it is dark.

Why dwell there?

You might ask, for I will answer, as dark as the earth, is the depth of my longing to love completely.

My heart has a rhyme, review and revelation without recourse or remorse with subtle palpitations a compilation of a rhythm from each beat of my life.

My heart lies beneath the earth where it is dark.

Where the earth is murky the ground is damp, mostly from the tears of my journey to you, for it has been long and not very sweet.

I am in awe of the timing that fate would have us to meet.

My heart lies beneath the earth where it is dark.

I HAVE HAD

I have had lots of loves but never the kind of love I wanted

It would be hot and I would be cold, it would be sad and I would be happy

I would be spontaneous it would be stale, I would be excited and it would be dull

I would be in discovery and it would be in Para-normal state

I would be listening and it would be silent

I would be speaking and it would be deaf

I would be Cheyenne or Aqua and it would be green or gray

I would be silver lightening and it would be cloudy on a clear day

I would be exhaling the warmth and it would be inhaling the cold

I would be shining moon beams of love and it would be engulfed in midnight's fog

I have had a lots of loves but none that knew me when

SHE DID IT WITH A FLASH
(for Ann Marsden)

We rushed eagerly, unsuspecting of what experience may lie ahead of us; simply, we walked into a moment, in time that awaited our arrival

We entered the studio on the right, with high vaulted ceilings and picturesque windows that allowed fractions of natural light to enter

At the meeting of our introduction the room was full with sun rays and rainbows full of marmalade, Immediate likeness and a melodic spirit cradled, each of us felt the energy level elevate,

She stood tall, elongated possibly by being dressed in all black attire with thin glasses sculpted around her face; she presented herself to us with such kindness, warmth, and grace

What wondrous energy and power she projects; it must be the ability to create striking images at the base of her fingertips, and inventive to be able to capture the creator's beauty within a glimpse of an eye and a shutters lens

She did it with a flash and I was a witness to perfection, the raw beauty my children's faces

She did it with a flash and blessed my heart

R.E.S.P.E.C.T.

Recognizing the heart

Enduring this life

Sharing your journey

Preparing for the future

Evolving beyond

your struggles

Cultivating your spirit

Tenacity to change

and

breaking the cycle

For the sir in my life

Safely

I found a warm calm spot

It was holding the fold of your arms

The heat from your body

Warms my heart

Without touches from you

I know I am safe

No need to fear you

For you are peace

Neither seeking, nor wanting

Just offering moments

Of company and conversation

Shallow volume

Slow moments with you

Fill the room

The echoes become silent

In your presence, I release

In resolve, I am with you

Only

Quietly, sweetly

I reside with you

I found my safe house

In your presence

SIR…

WHEN DADDY LEFT

What I really needed but never got

I wanted someone to comfort me, but no one was there

No one was willing to witness my pain

I wanted someone to hold me and tell me everything was going to be All Right but there were no arms strong enough

No one was willing to acknowledge my loss

I wanted someone to hear my reverberating thoughts,

but there were no ears big enough

to handle what I needed to say

No one was willing to share my load

I wanted someone to soften my fall from grace

but there was no one to catch me

No one was willing to shoulder my sorrows

I only wanted someone to be strong for me so I could be weak for just

Once.

My Pocket

I put your heart in my pocket

I never stopped loving you

I just tucked my heart away

So your eyes could not see

I put our hearts in my pocket

I tried so hard to bury those feelings

Then you found me

Reached in my pocket

And unlocked my heart with your key

Only to find out you still loved me

I never stopped loving you

I only stuff our love in my

Back pocket

THEY PUMP ME UP

I love my bad ass red shoes

I am taller, sexier and even more flexible

I feel like a damn superhero

Going out with my sister girls

With my bad ass red shoes on

Where's my cape and cat suit

Cause I have on 4 inch heels

Tall, lengthy and luscious

Straps at my ankles

Bold yes brazen

Jewels at my toes

The heels are sheer

Hard for the naked eye to see

Damn I love these heels as

Much as my man loves me

They make me feel like a million

On a Saturday night

I love my bad ass red shoes

Cuz they make me feel

Alright!

Section Four

Reverberations (Echos)

Passion,
Suffering
Powerful
Feelings

The Best Gift

The best gift you ever gave me was the day you decided to leave me.

It was the best gift you ever gave me!

You gave me my life back

You gave me my laughter back

You gave me pain, but it went away

You gave me my spirit back

You gave me my strength back

You gave me fear, but I learned to have faith

As I stood in the face of uncertainty

You gave me my heart back

You gave me my love back

Now I can use it to heal myself

You gave me the truth back

You gave me my motherhood back

Now I do not have to explain why I choose her over you

You gave me my pride back

You gave me my title and respect back

Queen and the ability to accept nothing less

You gave me my freedom back

You gave me my independence back

Now I am free to share my talents with the world

You gave me my style and grace back

You gave me my spontaneity back

For I truly love life without you in it

The best gift you ever gave me was letting go because I could not find the strength to do it myself

So, I thank you!

BIRTHED

Oh how I love life wanting to deliver this thing that is within me, etched deep in my souls womb a dwelling that moves and motions greatness the ebbing and flowing that carries

Will God let you emerge and enter this realm, the baby I have wanted has taken a long time, painful process but I know souls deep that its time it must come

So I see that you use one wounded and the other dead, but I see so many dreams delayed, dismayed, made crooked when thought to be straight

Alone and unwelcome thoughts on a journey the truth pierces like the cold wind tearing abruptly at my cheeks

Demanding that I answer the hollowing of the wind with a decision I thought I could never make, would never make

How could I walk with pain of this existence that was never meant to be, me knowing I would forever be changed by natures call to me and to the world

Quiet moments with house notes written on the walls of my heart never to be forgotten never to be revealed knowing I would not get the opportunity to forgive what I surrendered even though I have birthed.

No Invitation Needed

I invited myself to dinner at your house

Because I think you are hiding something

Yes, I would like candied yams, rice, corn bread and baked chicken with gravy

Then you have the nerve to ask me if

I would like some sweet tea (T)

You know, I have not seen that Negro since, the last sunset kissed my hips and

Washed my lips with molasses

Don't ask me any more damn questions

I invited myself, to dinner because I think you are hiding something

What are you afraid of?

I only want your love and friendship

But you will not let me, I enjoy sitting with you, talking

When I am with you I feel safe and warm as if I were cocooned by you,

Can you hear what I am saying?

I invited myself to dinner because I think, you are hiding something,

I think it is good loving and I want you to let me in

Sir, will you let me into your heart, your

Music, and your love

I invited myself to dinner because I love you, I do not want you to hide anymore

RIGHTEOUS ANGER
(thanks to Elder, Ms. Josie Johnson)

I may not be able to speak up for myself sometimes But I always will stand in the gap for my fellow "wo" man

I may not be the best fighter or the strongest person But I will defend someone else being bullied even if I have to run

I may not know all the laws of the land or all of my inalienable rights But I know when I see injustice, I believe it is pointed directly at me

I may not hold any of the 1 % of wealth in this country but I believe that each of us should be treated as though we are worth more than a million bucks and I do not mind standing in the hole for someone less fortunate

As a matter of fact, I have righteous anger and I think it is my duty to use it to fuel the fire to advocate for others

Therefore, I stand for children who cannot comprehend maltreatment but need a vanguard, I stand in the trenches for parents who may not understand all the rules that govern them and I stand in the fissure for elders who have given the best years of their lives so I can stand on their shoulders.

I may not be the smartest or most educated on any particular topic, but I come from a long line of strong Black women who were not afraid to let their righteous anger be known to those who hold power and more importantly those who abuse it.

I stand here humbly not because I was chosen by anyone but because I was called to help and not hurt, to affirm and not degrade, to support and not judge, to guide and not deter for this righteous anger governs me where ever I go.

As a matter of fact, I have righteous anger and I think it is my duty to use it to fuel my fire to advocate for others

I may not win every battle I choose to enter, but I believe it is better that I was willing to stand up and speak up for what I believe are undeniable truths and let my righteous anger be known.

Why she hurts

Why be who she's not

Why become

When all she does is cry

Weeping for her true self

Suffering in expectations

Visions of everyone else's view

Longing to free her self

In word, deed and truth

Why be when everyone

Has such a shallow view

Release her from your narrow version

In the shadows of you

Hiding from others

Camouflaging your words and actions

Admit it!

You have never noticed me because

I dare to be the Authentic ME!

Dear Lover

She is the lover you sleep with nightly but you never really knew!

I am writing to you from the me you cannot touch with your hands or see with your eyes. I am speaking from the soul that lies deep within me, the one you have not had the pleasure of meeting her acquaintance.

Although, you may have lain beside inside her, you never touched the true essence of her being or her earth, the center of her universe, the inedible innermost, omni- present, untouchable core of who she truly is or who she was at that moment with you.

They often say we fake, we scream unnecessarily, when we boost egos and lie while lying sideways or on our backs, but the truth is we are never really touched until we let you in!

Yes, let you in inside the tomb which holds the womb of a spirit of a woman which houses her dreams her ambitions, her fear disappointment, her trials and her triumphs, her obstacles that she's overcome, her struggles and her strides her glows and her grows. Where she is where she came from and where she intends to be tomorrow.

You see there is truly more to be than what you've merely held in your hand at one time or another, I asked you do you dare, do you care to really touch me, to know is to owe and the exchange is truly giving of yourself and unless you have arrived at the same place I am at with you should not be touching me really at all.

Lover, to touch me is to owe, by loving me from the inside out.

When Love Calls

When love calls some say, you better answer, but I say if I hear you knocking, I may not let you in…

Love comes in the form of a bouquet and leaves in a hearse

It brings sunshine on a rainy day and leaves in clouds on a gloomy day

It brings smiles and laughter and leaves tears and pain

It brings hope and promise and leaves doubt and dismay

It brings roses and candy and leaves scars and wounds

When love calls and does not answer, now you know why

Autumn's Blues

I cannot sleep so many thoughts running through my head

I get up and put pen to paper or keys to keyboard just to release

The racing, running, leaping images of the world that I have captured in my mind

Sometimes I wonder have I truly lost it this time

I can't hear all of my thoughts because they are jumbled and scarce

I hear rhythms and sounds of past lives, dreams died and the endless hopelessness

My arms, my neck, my spirit are so restless

Sometimes I wonder to myself what I have done to contribute to the world's mess

I cannot see the silver lining in the sky I have to admit sometimes I feel blind

I mean I see young children, new babies and young graduates too but

My spirits screams what are these poor children going to live, experience and more importantly go through

Sometimes, I wonder am I doing enough to encourage the generation after X

That is vexed and perplexed, the ones that no one knows what to do next

For them

I cannot enjoy my mother's JAG, Cachupa or delicious stew dinners to taste

See she is gone, I know it was her time, but I miss her and she cannot be replaced

This strong lady judged not, lifted up the weary, fed the hungry, talked to the lonely, cared for the careless, pushed the weak, and encouraged the strong, No she was not perfect but she tried to right wrongs

Many of today's children have not tasted the meals of a parents love and

we often wonder what they are made of

I cannot say I have touched as many children as I need in my present life, but I try to not let an opportunity slip by. I get emotional, cry and sometime weep because I was raised with three generations of love that gave many affirmations to me

Stand by my side, no more sleepless nights because we want to sit back and holler as another child dies, sometimes physically by gunfire or drugs, I am talking about that child you see that feels unlovable and simply needs hugs.

Use your God given senses to touch, see and hear the needs

of the children today, they may not be yours but they have crossed your path for some reason

Extend beyond your temple to exalt another and be the first step on their journey to hope and purpose

And if you can't hear me or help me just help to stop my sleepless nights

Just Call Me Mysty

Tinkle, drip, drop, splish, splash

Rain , pour, gush, swish splash

I am done

Just call me mysty for I am filled with sweet sorrow for all the loves that could have been, should have been, those that were lost, those thrown away, and the ones who were simply shown to the door marked EXIT

Just call me mysty, for I am saddened by all the time wasted, minutes, hours, days, months, years and ultimately the "TIME" is all you have left to claim, not a supreme love, but moments, fragments, pieces of a dream

Just call me mysty for I grieve for the pain that lingers within me, tears, sighs, silent cries, screams that will never know sound, with every moan and ache there is a corpse of a love lost

Just call me Mysty

Drips and drops in puddles of loves lost

Broken Wing

Black swan, your wing span is wide, the strokes startle and your embrace is one of sultry movements with grace

You mesmerize and tantalize with your sweetness, it suffocates as feelings of ecstasy cloak me,

I lose sight and oxygen leaves my body simultaneously the other swan takes her last breath,

She begins to sink slowly, even graciously into the afterlife

(Pause)

Naw, I am just a black girl with a broken wing, see I have been through many things

See each time I am ignored, abused or disregarded, I can feel the particles of my heart separate from my soul

Departed, disconnecting the valve from the aorta, I realize that I am made strong to overcome the pain

I have been overtaken by the Black Swan, for she lives in me, but I am just a strong black girl with a broken wing!

Speak to Me

Speak to me Lord, Speak to me

Speak through me, I want to hear your voice, talk to me Lord, the way only you can, Lord do with me what you will, for I am your child

I am one that still needs you, with every step I make and each breath I take, only you and you alone can make me whole, only you Lord know which way I should go

Lord, precious Lord take both my hands, help me to walk in your way, help me to stand tall, when I am going to fall down on my face

Lord lift me up, I need you more than ever, Lord it is me in the need of prayer, I am standing here before you, with my arms stretched out, Lord my heart is open wide to receive you, with patience and persistence I will honor you,

Lord, Speak to me

Windows Pain

Looking out my windows pain

I see broken hearts and cracked lives

I hear long whispers that come from loud screams from deep inside

What do you see from your windows pain?

I feel heart aches of children and the emptiness of children where love does not live

I feel the anger of our community's children who do not know how to trust or give

What you see from your windows pain

I see no laughter, joy, happiness only pain, not on adults or grown men, these are the feelings of hopelessness on the minds of the children

Looking out of your windows pain from your corporate desk or dining room table in your high rise, do not ignore the pain in children's eyes.

While you look out of windows pain

Mirrored Image

I am an illusion to you and you don't even know it. I control the images that you see, it is a mask I wear, it is not really me

I am a sun catcher, you only see what shines through true parts of me which is withheld only if you knew

I lavish in my deception for it grants me power and control the world I created and I vow to uphold

I lost her many years ago, she lives no more it is superficial, artificial, and just plain fake but it is what I have done to survive and it is my sanity at stake

So look at me, even smile because the image you see only lasts a short while

I am a mirror with window panes of water splashes like the rain, I am a puddle you may step in, I am the ocean you swim whatever you can see there is a tiny little piece of me

So the next time you are at a crosswalk don't be afraid to look at me in the approaching traffic.

Section Five

NEW LENSES

A New Reign

No Thank You

Please baby!

No Thank you!

I thought I wanted it (you)

But now I changed my mind

I think I should let it go (the thought)

I smelled your aroma

And wanted you

To sit with me

Badly and sweetly

But then when I listened

No soft whispers dwelled

My heart said yes

But my head said no

No thank you

Please!

It's Pouring

Pouring pouring of my soul empty everything that got put in and all that others dumped on me emptying all the pollutants that discarded my soul like paperless weights drifting through time, pouring out one's struggles emptying the shadows and the frowns of others discomfort and disbelief owning

POUR from the place where you stand upon the rock God called for you to make residence on high purpose power and destiny, God does no pour empty promises into us he is the potter with divine directions and approval he is clear with precise prescriptions and plans Jeremiah 29:11 he had a purpose just for each of us to pour into on out of so that we may model his example of love compassion and encouragement into the hurt broken damaged abused and confused it is time to draw on God's well

And pour to your brother and sister offer grace mercy forgiveness and hope for the love of GOD we may never master but we can die trying please pour with me pour with me cry unto the Lord and pour with me the grace that you have not been given pour with me the promises that have been broken pour with me the lies that have been told and that have traveled pour Pour GOD is at the WELL.

SHE LOOKS LIKE A LADY

Act like a Woman, but look like a lady,

I sat next to this sharp lady in a chocolate brown suit, short sculpted hair, pointed glasses that matched her shoes.

As the bus maneuvered corners and hills she sat motionless, it was like her eyes never blinked, not for a second

As we approached the final stop as the bus entered the station I put forth my arm extending to motion you may go first.

Without looking in my direction actually never noticing me she said, "No Thank YOU"

I followed her down the corridor, up the stairs and on to the platform, never noticing I missed my exit from the station I sat wondering her name

I motioned again this time trying to sell her some old pumps that had been worn by my many other women in various stages of their discovery with cookie crumbs still in the toe of the shoe

She only put out one finger to say, "STOP, Don't move another inch, I am not the average lady but 110% Woman"

"I'm not interested in the trip you are selling, not the vacation in Malibu, I've been where you are wanting to go and my final answer Blind Man is, No Thank YOU

I act like a lady and I think like a WoMAN…

With a Thankful Heart

When I opened my eyes this morning, I knew I needed to pray to start my day and I thought of you friend in a special way. I pray each step we take today may it be blessed, I pray you speak words of love when you are faced with a test. May your patience for others be long and meek, please help others who seem to be strong but deep down inside they may feel weak. I pray you hear God's sweet whisper in your inner ear so that you don't miss the small miracles I know will appear. I hope my prayer has touched your heart today to love and serve another in a special way. Be blessed my friend is all I wanted to say. Maybe it was just me that needed to share my morning prayer with thee. Perhaps, I needed to take a minute with God and give him reverence for all he has done for me.

You'll Learn My Name

Sometimes she's so rough, her skin feels like scales to the touch of a males caress

she has the most welcoming smile that speaks volumes before her sweetest words bless your ears

but one cross of the tongue will present lack of knowledge for your first offense

the venom meets your indiscretion with fierce ocean walls

see how quickly her silky embrace turns

her once smooth sheath that allured the feelings that were emitted from the most sincere

as she sheds her covering those feelings of silk turn into leather with a blink of the eye

she is strong as an ox but she is not one to exert the true will of her force, the clutch will send you into a subconscious daze that will leave you more than speechless

she is far more precious than rubies or gold

when she leaves, you will be more than remiss, but the beauty of her movements draws you in, yet again she acts with such precision and grace it makes most men halt and succumb to an immobile state of shock

Love is her choice of weapons but the power is in every stroke that she lies on your brow with her head upright in an erect position, she stares deeply into your soul for the truth and when it is absent or diminished, she recognizes the emptiness and she strikes not for your mouth to settle the score but she strikes the eyes, for you will never witness her pain of realizing that this love is gone forever.

For she only desires to be called by her proper name "deah reppoc"

Tempting Temptations

No's become Yes's and a quiet storm looms overhead, long sighs turn into deep exhales and twilight meets your sunrise

Tempting

Beckoning, summoning your presence, thoughts turn in to fantasies and doubts become possibilities and actions yield reality

Temptation

Safe distance no longer arm's length and your spatial sense is eroded by your willingness to surrender to the secrets

Tempting

Bones ache, arches entangle your once calm demeanor into a calculated stupor that leads and responds without reason, Just rock in the rhythm

Temptation

Roads less traveled but you often pass many with frequent flyer miles, who cannot begin to tell you how they succumbed to the sultry abyss

Tempting

Tread cautiously as you entertain moving, the sweetness of memories and deep desires that welcome deception, it's hard to resist and easy to indulge in your

Tempting Temptations.

IF

If I were to die tonight, what would you say about me, If I asked you to speak at my funeral or write my eulogy, what words would you use, when you thought of me

Kisses of kindness or swift words that break branches, or calm colloquialisms, that describe my personality, would you welcome the opportunity to serve my children with an apron of love and comforting words in their time of sorrow would you share small morsels of their mom to help them through tomorrow

If I were to die tonight I wonder who would cry for me, for moments we will never have or time we wanted to spend again, but didn't, not in splendor, no need for sorry or forgive me, no moments or gifts you will never give to me.

If I were to die tomorrow, I would want you to hold my hand dear friend and say you will continue to walk remembering me, I would want my lover to love me like it is the last time, provide me with a new level of ecstasy, I would hug my children and never let go and tell them no matter if I am near or far I would never let them feel the cold (of life)

If I were to die tomorrow, I would want you to give me my roses today.

IF (II)

If I were to die tomorrow, what would I say to you?

I would tell you first it is ok

I would say everything will be all right

I would tell you how much I love you

I would say, Thank you for gracing me with your presence, truth, visions and journey, absence of your deception.

I would tell you those little things that use to bother me don't matter any more

I would tell you to not sweat the small things or people, you have too many big fish to stir fry and move on

I would tell you to make a real plan for your life and do not deviate from its course

I would say hold on to scriptures Jeremiah 29:11 and Psalms 121, which are scriptures for my life

I would say pray frequently and often, put the Lord on autopilot

God will grant your desires; you must work hard to fulfill your dreams because the disasters will come

I would tell you I am sorry, because I know I have caused you some pain

I would say please forgive me and release your heart from any affliction I may have caused

I would say try to live your life by treating everyone with peace, patience, kindness and respect, things I tried to improve

I would say earnestly live your purpose daily; you were made to accept nothing less

Anything worth having and living is worth dying, if you leave the world a little brighter and sweeter to the taste, you have shared your special flavor with humanity

I would say I know I am leaving way too soon but you all know you were loved the best way I knew for the time I was given

Then I would say, you may miss me, but keep me in your heart and make me proud by fulfilling your dreams, serving others and helping a child make it in this cruel world

I would say please bless my children and husband with your love and compassion give to them tenfold what I have given you during my stay. Remember them long after I am gone, after the high praise service and dried flowers, they will need you most then

Always remember to trust God even when you do not understand, just trust and obey because there is no other way to find harmony

Good-bye for now and I hope to be with you again, I pray I will see your face smile upon me on Heaven's Hillside.

Fortress in a Dress

I cover, I conceal at the same time I reveal a small piece of me, who will take heed, who will walk on by never noticing me, like the wind I am omnipresent

I AM A FORTRESS IN A DRESS

I make myself invisible to the naked eye

I shield my heart from the world

I bury my spirit

I camouflage my thoughts

I AM A FORTRESS IN A DRESS

I drape my conscience in tapestry

I dance my words into song

I speak of freedom trapped

I write lyrical truths clothed in poetry

I AM A FORTRESS IN A DRESS

My walls are high and deep

My shadows are dark and gray

My door is closed and kept shut

Because I do not like the company knocking

FOR I AM A FORTRESS IN A DRESS

Autumn's Spring

The spring rain drops

Drape the breast of my cheek bones

These tear drops are mine

A Poem for the Wounded

I give love to the wounded person just like me

I pray for the wounded that may be blind but wants to see

I reach out to the wounded to hold because I know the power of a real hug

I listen to the wounded because everyone needs to be heard and more importantly loved.

For the student who weeps but never sheds tears

For the student who fights with brute force to cover her fears

For the student who hides in class because no one sees them as the promise of our future

For the student who demands attention by yelling because no one witnesses their pain

For the tiniest student whose sorrow we will never know

I OFFER YOU

I offer you your heart back that you can uplift and hold tight and for every wrong you can choose to make it right

For your heart is your strongest organ and weapon god gave you as a gift

You can use your heart to love a friend and uplift and hold them high

You can use your heart to comfort a sister who needs to cry

You can use your heart to listen to those who have never known support

You can use your heart to see beyond anyone's faults and serve their needs

You can use your heart to touch someone who has never been accepted

You can use your heart to encourage those who were told they were no good and rejected

See this poem is for my wounded students that I love who may not know their love heals my wounds every day for they are me.

Reflection

The game of life can sometimes be funny

It deals cards from a stacked deck

It offers monopoly money and then tells you to pay your all your debts

I often look out of stained filled windows into the gray skies

You may wonder how can I see the sun through rain

How could I appreciate rainbows?

When I only feel pain

How can I sing and dance in the street

When I left my heart in the cemetery

It is the reflection from which I see

The beauty, the hope of learning to live my true destiny

Rebirth

I have arrived

I have overcome

I have been to the mountain top

I have had time to enjoy the view

I am so very lucky to have the opportunity to say

I have been born again

And I do not walk the way I use to walk

I do not talk the way I use to talk

I do not go the places I use to go

I have a new lease on life

And

I am so happy to be

Born again

Please do not stand in the way of the sun,

Oops, sorry that's just my

Glow!

Sweet Peace

Is a place deep within your spirit, it sleeps with pillows from heaven, it snores with angels on high, it rests in knowing that there is a better place, and the reward is resting on the promise!

Sister Without a Name

Clinched jaw holding back the pain, weeping inside as if pouring rain was drowning the heart floating inside her body, thoughts overwhelm as if there are waves and winds drenching her peace

She desperately clings with one finger to a piece of thread as it strips from the palm of her hand, moments of silence engulf her spirit holding as she reaches for herself within

She releases and exhales, Jesus I know you dwell here, you lie within the pandemonium you separate all her jumbled thoughts making my words clear

As she cries her tears drip, drench, stream to her cheeks as she weeps for thee, she knows where her help and promise lies, within your midst dear Jesus

She has stumbled yet again on the same rock that has been in her path 100 times, she has gone down in your holy name but somehow she cannot leave her flesh, her weakness, her greed, her petty ways behind her

These doubts are earthly, womanly and in them, she fights, struggles because she does not want to lose sight of the calling of her life to lead and serve her name is Nicole and genuine is her heart, servant are her hands, hopeful are her eyes, truth bounds from her lips as her spirit aches to fulfill her desire knowing she was called not chosen by anyone but you Lord, on one June day you decided that I would live an abundant life with your mark etched upon my breast

Lord awesome Father and ruler I am victorious and wondrous Glory,

You gave me a new name and it is BLESSED

Walking Across My Mind

You walked across my mind today and left a trail of footprints on my heart

Your presence awakened in me those feelings I thought I buried deep down inside

With each step my heart made me remember what I have tried so hard to forget

I tilted my head to the left hoping to stop what my heart was saying to my mind, that you were walking around like you were home; those footprints on my heart were being felt deeper than I remember the first imprints of you

I moved again because this was uncomfortable and you were not welcome anymore because love with you does not reside here, she moved on a long time ago

You walked across my mind today and left a trail of footprints on my heart, I tilted my head to the left and I began to fall apart, it caused me to remember what I chose to forget

You walked across my mind today and it reminded me of so many regrets.

Again You Walked

You walked across my mind today and then you stayed there and I began to remember how we use to be, how sweet we laughed, played and laid together

You walked across my mind today and then you parked yourself on my heart and it began to beat hard and fast, then I remembered what we use to do, when we laughed, played and laid and how we stayed glued together

You walked across my mind today and your presence was felt by every inch of me then I remembered how we use to touch, kiss and love each other

You walked across my mind today and the vision of you was of your lips, shoulders thighs and back and then I remember what was yours was mine

You walked across my mind today and a deep echoing of sadness filled me and I could not hold back the tears for you, felt by my heart's wishes and longs for the ecstasy of yesterday's gone

You walked across my mind today and I wished you were right here just so I could let you in!

Section Six

Truth serum

Nothing
But the
Truth

Truth Serum, the Truth about Lies

The truth about lies is in your eyes, it is your hair, in our bodies, imprinted, touching us everywhere here in lies the festival of lies

Art blends and synergizes a synthesis of threads weaving truth with lies and lies with truth not knowing whose truth or story is being told

Censored Art is not a lie but truth revealed in creative display, True art is truth with a splash of lies beautifully distorted with a personal view

Lemons or propaganda is a lie celebrated when truth is designed in the form of art

There is always the lie in confidence of how to walk, where to dine, what we say, when you are drinking, perhaps

We all find time to give honor to the festival of lies

Do you even know when I say, Yes, I love you, or am I really saying, NO I DO NOT

Is it the house or your religious beliefs that trickle the truth out about the pastor, is he the real thief?

Mr. Master, Honorable, Constable, Lover of Friends, when will the lies we lead come to an end

Shuttle, Explorer or aero plane, how much truth do we tell before a lies slips in again?

How much truth is said in what you say?

Ain't That a Bitch…

I gave you what you wanted and you said, it was too soon. Ain't that a bitch…?

I love you with all the love I have to give and you said, it was not good enough. Ain't that a bitch…?

I give to you without you asking, or expecting in return, because I want you to have all that you need, however, when I am in need, I have to ask. Ain't that a bitch…?

I am not your girlfriend, I am not your wife and I am not your mistress but you still lie to me. Ain't that a bitch…?

I wonder if you even tell yourself the truth, because if you don't, I would say to you, ain't that a bitch…?

Visits

Your visits startle me

Even though I know you are always lurking

When you show up unexpectedly

You steal my joy in broad day light

Stripping my smile from my heart and face

I pray someday it will be the last day you pay me a visit

I wish our paths never crossed on that day

I would have been fine with you

Sure I will recognize your type next time

I must be sure not to let an imposter in to my precious peace

Again.

When I Reflect

I watch the waves in the water and wonder why they are traveling in that way, is it because of the wind, but at a moment's notice, I see an area of water moving in the opposite direction no matter a sea, river, lake or stream the force of water is something like life and love

Sometimes too strong, at times too gentle and it is never noticed or just then there is a calm harmonic motion and this is the serene meeting, making peace

In life I aim to travel a course of certainty and purpose, but many times I find that I have veered way off course traveling this road was unforeseen, I had been warned of these same lessons I thought were learned, but I tread the water anyway, the wisdom of the scribes had written on the walls, and yes I continue to move steadily down the path because why I wondered asking myself, why

No tears for my yesterday's they were meant to be as they were and that is why I am, I have faith that someday all that I have experienced will transform my soul into one that is wise and true, to thyself and others, I will be able to do this because I will have no fear

For the Love of Tea

Toasting, drinking, testing new flavors aromas pleasantly kissing my nose while sanctifying my chemo senses with warm vapors, charming my senses alluring me to what I love most

The molecules and meeting of my taste buds and tongue, welcoming micro-spices and herbs massaging the crevices of my mouth, awakening endings of sensory with caresses of honey, chamomile and vanilla, whispering sweet nothings to my brain, introducing images stroking my hard and soft palate

What a wonder I experience undertaking the romance I have with TEA, see we have been together for over thirty years and I must say even through the hard times, he never left my side, always letting me know there was a warm place I could come home to, see even when I was feeling the brash winds of life's roller coaster

I would be beckoned to the new quiet peaceful place of Chai, see he was boldly flavorsome, challenging me to pay close attention to its detail and delight, ginger, cinnamon, and cardamom, blessing me with fiery bursts, it is enlightenment to my soul, summoning me to savor the full experience while dancing with the many sugar cubes in my cup that have now traveled to my head

This love affair with tea, will not end for I cannot deny him in the spring, winter, and fall, for with him is where I choose to be and knowing that each meeting is like fresh spearmint in my soul with 10,000 tantalizing tenants engulfing me with a little bit heaven in my tea cup.

Your Box

This box you put me in does not fit

As a matter of fact

It's not me at all

It has harsh edges, sharp crevices and

Abrupt ends

Where is my whistle?

I would like to blow it,

Freeze this pane,

This Motion picture must end!

I do not want the starring role in this movie

It was created for someone else

It limits my scope, my purview

And it traps my inner beauty,

You can have this box it does not fit!

Autumn's Fall

See, I love nature and

I have been admiring God's

Cotton Candy Skies

But little did I know

I was caught by the twinkle in your eyes

Cautious of show and tell

All while you tell me

You can walk through water

And not get wet

But can you dance with me in puddles

And not get mud on your shoes

You say I might like it

Getting muddy with you…

KISSING ME

The sun kisses my skin on this Tuesday morn

Not harshly but sweetly

It tastes vanilla in my hue

And before you know it

I am as golden as you

Sweetly the sun kisses me

From head to toe

It savors my skin even

As the wind blows

Gently it covers me with

A blanket, a glove

The sun feels so good it

Must be love

CAN YOU FORGIVE ME

If you knew I did not mean to break your heart, would you forgive me and move on with love

Can you forgive me; There is nothing, I would not do to ease the pain, I have caused, but I am not sure

what can I do to make things right

Our love was imperfect with many flaws and blemishes; we were always a work in progress

Can you forgive me; I know we were not growing as one, sitting and dealing maybe, but not loving effortlessly

I never said loving me would be easy, nor did I say understanding me would be any easier, but the love I gave you is eternally yours

Can you forgive me; and accept what I did was best, I am not throwing away all the love we had, I am just discarding everything less than the sum of 360 degrees of love we once had

I could not live my life subtracting and depleting the abundance of love we shared, no more responses about setbacks, shortcomings, I just could not stand by your side anymore loving you the way I have

Can you forgive me and move on with love because I would not allow limits on our love, and in doing so I chose to walk away

Our Daily Bread

When are we going to mourn together?

So many silent cries in our rooms

Alone we cry out at the same time

We cry for our mother

As each day passes

We hide the pain more and more

From one another from ourselves

The pain is there deeply rooted

Anchored, etched in our hearts

The loss

Hugs we need that we will never get

Once again we suffer alone

Because we are afraid to share the pain

The acknowledgement will make it real

We are afraid of the pain inside

We truly are one

We must remember

Her love

(Trudy)

NOT KINDNESS OR WEAKNESS

I will not apologize for my love and kindness in the wake of rejection and disregard

Yes, I can still want to love and take care of you even if you have no compassion left for me

I've been told I am a fool even stupid for having the willingness to lift you up when you fall. I will hold your hand when you are afraid to pay attention all while paying debts when you care nothing for me

Yes, I have even wept asking God to take away my sensitivity for others plights and struggles because many times there have been no ears or arms big enough to hold me

In the sweetest whisper in the wake of my tumultuous storms, God said,

"dear child do not weep or mourn over anything or who you are because it means you are closest to me

Being willing to shoulder someone's burdens is one of the greatest gifts you could give me, rejoice child for you are never alone, for you are with me, never apologize or forsake."

"Tell them while they laugh or squander what you give them, have no fear or doubt stand boldly knowing it is the Jesus in me!"

I will feed the hungry and shelter the lonely, I will love the unlovable and help the hopeless, I will guide the lost and speak for the mute

No I will not apologize for my kindness because Jesus, said it ain't so.

Job 6:14, Job 10:12, Isaiah 63:7, Jeremiah 9:24 and Jeremiah 31:3

You won't make me over but he will

Feelings, some of us have too much of them others don't have enough, some of us wear them on our sleeves, some on our chest, so you can't see it

How can I put my trust in you, how can I learn to trust another man with my heart the only man I know who can take it and won't break it, IS Jesus

Then again, he is not a Natural Man, is he?

Yes I have been bruised but not beaten, I have been hurt but not destroyed, I have been changed but not remolded

The changing I desire now is made by GOD let him create in me a new tapestry for life let him design the new me with ordered steps by his word accompanied with wisdom and not without understanding.

God I pray someday my feelings will be understood

Stormy Monday

See today is stormy Wednesday but he said I look like a MONDAY on this day, you can't help but lose

So, what I lost today was my man and three kids and a fish tank (smile)

Yeah, this is not a just can't say good bye poem, what it is however

Is the flubber meeting the float well they both sank…To the bottom of one's list of who is on first and who will get first

What I desire is the wind being beneath my wings and the sun's rays blessing me

See I am a Stormy Monday who needs the energy and power of nature's presence to carry me through my next journey in life

The plans are to carry out all that GOD has prospered me and only I can do this, I welcome and feel very blessed to embark on the true path that I was meant to travel

Far beyond where I have dared to go thus far, much deeper than I was willing to tarry and higher than my eyes can see

Turmoil is part of my nature because my heart's desire is to be loved and not possessed, to be cared for but not carried, to be listened to and not instructed, for the wisdom I have is ancestor birthed and spiritually tuned

Storms of wind and rain in my life have always been on Monday but revelation has always been delivered on a SUNNY SUNDAY afternoon…

Changing Lanes

I choose to go this way by choice

I want to put my blinker on and change lanes right here,

This lane is moving a little faster and it is going in the direction I desire to go,

This lane is paved, smooth and the white lines are clearly in my view,

My night blindness does not even affect me anymore.

This is an impromptu road trip I was supposed to take at this point in time and

I know this path is going to lead me to my true destiny

He's No Cupcake

He is the sweetness between her lonely days and nights

He is the one she calls to lift her spirits when she is weary and unsure

He is there when you disappoint her and push her away

She calls him to keep her warm until you let her back in

Do you know who he is, well I will tell you

He is her krème fill'in

He loves her when you're not available

He takes her out when you are gone

He listens to her when you choose not to hear her thoughts

He shows her sensitivity when you cannot feel

He buys her gifts you wish you could give her

She shares her fantasies with him because with him they become a reality, but once again

Do you know who he is, well I will tell you

He is her krème fill'in

Oh yes, do you understand

She has your sir name

She bore your children

She lives her life with you

Yes, you get all the rewards of his labor

Shit, your relationship is even better because of him

He will never get what he has put in

But nevertheless while your too busy

He is her Kreme Fill'in

I GUESS YOU DID NOT KNOW

I did not know you leaving me would hurt you so bad

When you told me you did not want me anymore, unfortunately it was not the first, second but the third time is a charm, so I thought finally you made up your mind and I could finally admit it too

Yes, it's over and now I will walk away knowing we tried our very best!

But the better days would be ahead without you,

The better days will be when I sleep alone, the better days will be not hearing your voice. The better days will be, not seeing your face. The better days will be, not hearing your lies, the better days will be, not witnessing your deceit, the better days will be, not pretending anymore!

Damn it, I guess I did not get it after all because I thought this is what you really wanted but a short time passed and I knew this was the best gift you ever gave me, you want to tell me how I F'd up?

And now I am the air you breathe, well I guess I should give you an application to Chartwell so they can set you up with your weekly oxygen deliveries because I have exhaled and inhaled every day you have been gone,

And I am doing just fine!

But what I do not understand is your bitterness towards me I mean I only gave you what you wanted but I guess you did not know leaving me would hurt you so bad!

So the better days you thought you would have did not come yet, huh,

You miss sleeping beside me, you really miss hearing my voice, you miss feeling my touch and you even miss seeing my face

You know what I even feel sorry for you and for the relationship that was just not meant to be,

But I must admit I am glad it is hurting you more than it's hurting me

You Loving Me

Yes, I wish you were here to love me in the snow

I would welcome you home to warm hugs and kisses, as I helped you take off your coat and hat. I would walk you over to the fire place and have you lie down on the pillows

You hot tea with honey and fresh baked muffins are right by your side, but before you can reach for your cup I begin to feed you slowly hand to mouth, lip to cup and the real sweets are lips to lips

Oh how I wish you were here to love me in the snow

I will just touch your face gently with my warm hands, for I have just dipped them in a bowl of warm water with vanilla oils, I first touch your forehead, cheeks and then I massage your temples in a circular motion, yes this is my way of making sure that you know you were missed

Oh how I wish you were here to love me in the snow

Now that you are warm and relaxed I will place your head in my lap and we will talk softly about your day and I will listen intently hanging on to your every word, absorbing all you need me to hear

I then lean over you to whisper in your ear how much I want for you to love me right now in the snow, how I need for you to love me in the afternoon hour until the midnight hour and then sunrise of the next day

Oh how I wish you were here to love me in the snow

I remember oh so well our winter wonderland and the vivid designs of us creating moments of pleasure on our slopes with ecstasy directing each movement as our insatiable appetites increased for the next level to be reached, attained and sustained for as long as we both could stand

I cannot help but remember how well we made love in the snow

Call Me Elsa

Wounded Mare

Wandered here

Could not find her way

Looking upon the hills

as her vision fails

Wounded Mare

Have no fear

Your journey will not be long

The path you trod is still in view,

Wounded Mare

Beautiful is your mane

No matter the distance

Your sheer power will carry you there

Oh how I love the

Wounded Mare

For she is a lioness at heart

Section Seven

BLACK ROSES

Black Men

Pretty Brown Penny

What do you think our children feel like?

A pretty brown penny, is what I say

No one wants them

Everyone throws them away

Too many of them is a nuisance (cents)

A pretty brown penny, is what I say

What do we say to our children?

One makes no cents (sense)

Two of them is still not enough

Three or more is too much of an expense (cents)

A pretty brown penny, is what I say

What do we show our children?

Green is more valuable than them

They have no place in America

We do not trust in GOD

Liberty will always be in front or behind

Them as long as their brown

You'll always be a an outsider in another

Man's house

Pretty brown penny, is what I say

Daddy

Oh how I miss you

Now that you are gone

Your tender kisses

On my cheek

Huge hugs

That were

Love filled

This little girl's

Heart still aches

Oh how I miss my

Daddy even though

I am all grown

Up

Daddy

I Still

Need you

No Room in the In

Isn't it ironic?

That there was no room

For JESUS in the inn

But there is room and sought occupancy

For my son, brother, nephew, husband

Uncle and father

Simply because of whom they are

African American

Men

Blindly we stand by and accept

Yet another one in three to become

Incarcerated because he acquires a higher

Storage fee

When investors can insist on 96% occupancy

I have to take a stand and say

I will not sit back and accept this silently

No room for JESUS, but plenty of room

For you

We have a new form of free of labor in

TWENTY ONE TWO…

BLACK ROSE

Black Rose stand strong and tall, for many of the forces will encourage you to fall.

Black Rose, there is always a sun with a beam of light to guide you through your gloomy days and your darkest night.

Black Rose, do not be fooled by the cunning smile or the small opportunities that exist for a short while

Black Rose, put your stake in life's ground do not let your indecision be the conqueror of your true destiny.

Black Rose, tomorrow waits for no one, today is sure to pass and yesterday is just a fading memory.

Black Rose, use your petal as shields for life's abundance of disappointments, let them protect you.

Black Rose, you are the seed of life for tomorrow that is feared by so many today.

The Black Man's Hands

(thanks to Winton Marsalis and the Lincoln Center Jazz Orchestra, MN 2/1998)

The hands of a Black Man can tell many stories, if you would study them you would see

I look at your hands Black Man and wonder what your life has been like

What they have experienced

What they have seen

What they have done

What they had to do

What were they forced to do

Oh Black Man I pray

Are they hands of Georgia or Sweet Savannah are they from the hills of Mississippi or straight from the delta

Are they hands from Alabama, Montgomery in fact, I value these Precious hands simply because they are Black

Black Man when I look at you, would you like to know what I see in the hands I study

I see hands of ebony that are round and powerful, I see hands of almond that have veins of steel which have labored, I see hands of mahogany that are sleek and skilled, I see hands of bronze that have manicured fingers that have instructed, I see hands of jet black that are muscular and inventive, I see hands of nutmeg, that have raised children with love, I see hands of pecan brown that are hard and nurturing, I see hands of bone that have created with insight and forbearance, I see hands of onyx that are firm and uplifting

The Black Man's hands have survived the unthinkable, the unimaginable and the unbearable, for this I pray we all remember that with the hands of the Black Man this great nation was built.

Maybe if we took time to survey the hands of our fellow Black Man, we would not judge so quickly!

America in Black

What do you see when you see my little black son smiling up at me.

I am overjoyed at the promise in his eye and filled with the love of his long stare but I would be lying if I did not tell you my heart is filled with fear

I will raise him with love, compassion and humility because it's a must to survive but he has no idea about the hatred that awaits him outside,

I teach and practice his lessons, I test because I know as he grows if he makes a mistake he will be taken, not missed, just one less, mother, I've always wanted to ask you, do you worry about the simplest things about your boy like I do?

When he reaches 2nd grade he is cute no more, when he goes to school or how he should act before he goes to the store and what about when he gets his license, too how to respond to the boys in blue because their principles alone could kill you

America in Black this is me trying to raise my son who is only three

I tell him he is free and can live the American dream but I am reminded daily, we are living and breathing America in Black

Heart Breaker

Sons gone off to war, yeah they are not home no more

Guns, fighting, knives and the steel, yeah these things are going on, this is their real deal

Heart Breaker, Sons are questioning what is this all about

Although they are living the day to day trying to figure it all out

They want to ask their daddy's or uncle's but there absent or gone

Nevertheless, they assume the role and their unmatched leadership is born

My nephew, dear nephews have to be the men of the family to help raise the girls

However, he still seeks the knowledge of leadership, he reaches out and instills

Heart Breaker

Because he knows, he is not the ideal role model but he continues to lead and the younger ones follow

He watches children, takes babies to the library and to the museum

He honors his ancestors and teaches the youngest the value of the black man

He stands, tall; He walks with an arch to his back, and looks you in the eye without ever looking back

See Heart Breaker in the eyes of their mothers because they know how he learned,

How did he learn all this when the father to son talks did not happen there were no tutorials or tell what to do's

As far as he remembered, it was mother and son against the world at first light and that is what we do

Heart Breakers are their sons

When two young men's greatest accomplishments has taken them away

We have smiles on our faces but our hearts desperately try erasing any etchings of the day you left our sides

See this is the pain that lies deeply in side

These young men spoke life to a family, read words and righted wrongs but this is not a slow jam in our brains

It is a sad song,

Our reality is too hard to face, harder to speak and of the hardest are the silent moments we must live

See these young men are giants in black suits because they possess power beyond measure, courage that is audacious and the most difficult reality is they loved beyond limits

Heart Breaker is our Fernandez Sons, The True MIB

Dark Angel

I am waiting on my angel to love me

He is one with arms as wings

He holds me tight

When the wind is blowing hard and fast

Just being close to him I know everything is going to be alright

I've been praying to God to bless my dark angel because he loves me so like no one else can

During my prayers last night I said a special prayer to God for sending me my husband

HE'S AN ANGEL

God gave me an angel

He chose him just for me

He knows when I am sad

And feels when I am unhappy

He's quite, soft spoken

And never expects anything in return

He's says, "I am just here for you"

Watch me and you will see

You will soon believe

You will learn

He says, "God sent you and Angel"

And no matter where you live

Or what you do

At your side I will always be

I will go far

For I accept my assignment as your

ANGEL

I AM NOT A STORY TELLER

Telling stories, I have never thought of myself as a story teller but when I enter "the Walker" a transformation happens and my many matrixes of identities comes clearly into view

The prism of my existence illuminates images and colors prelude radiating off of others reflecting streams of light in the room

Then suddenly the textured layers of faces without names become a harvested room of plenty many telling stories of lack or visions that were not their own but then they too share their story, the undeniable moment when they WERE

Became the artist inside that body that was made to dance sing, paint, express, draw, create, write, scream and bleed.

See this story telling is serious business, not for the faint hearted but the strong willed, willing to become a teller of stories, and a listener of community and a heart without judgment and it is in this space on this particular night that I understand that I am now a Citizen of "the Walker!"

In remembrance of the late Sekou Sundiata,

Daddy's Ray's

Sunset on daddy

I miss your strong loving arms

See you in Heaven

Section Eight

FAMILY

Building
Upon
Legacy

Where love is concerned

Love is love but your mind is your OWN. Never love anyone more than you love yourself.

Respect the mind God gave you and do not give it to anyone to misuse where love is concerned.

BY: Gerald Vito Diggs, "DADDY"

Natural flowing hair

Hair is free

So let it be

Let it shine

All night

Let it sway

Like the waves

Hair is free

So let it be

By Justice J. Randolph age 9

RACE CAR

I am a race car

It's fast its cool

You can see the engine too

Two big wheels in the front

Two little wheels in the back

Speedy fast

Red, Yellow, Green and Gold

Silver

Speedy fast

Speed racer

By Malcolm M. Randolph age 7

Music

Its fast, it's slow

Its rock and roll

Its rhythm and blues

Its heart and soul

Its music to my ears

Its Jazz and Pizzazz

Its Music

By Justice J. Randolph age 9

Ode to Ma'ter

My light, my half, my rock, my friend, my cheerleader and my toughest critic, but the thing that describes you best is my mother. You have always been the epitome of strength and furthermore a role model for me throughout my life. In all the notes you wrote me when I was away, you always said I was your gift and inspiration, but mom in actuality you are my gift and my inspiration! As we gather here today for your 43th birthday anniversary I'm going to speak on how much you mean to me. You raised me, you love me, you give me advice and you continue to be there for me. I am eternally grateful for being blessed with a mother like you. Mom I love you happy birthday.

By Jazzmin B. Brooks Age 19

My Dope Fiend Father

My father was a "Dope Fiend"

I fiend to be a "Dope Father"

My Father was the man

Who use to pass me the bottle

And let me get a swig

Until I learned how to swallow

Like the "Role Models"

I use to want to follow

My insides corroded

Until I was hollow

But these are the men I use to want to follow

My father was a "Dope Fiend"

I Fiend to be a "Dope Father"

By L. Maurice Martin, A.K.A. "Pain"

My Soul Is On Fire

My soul is on fire

I traded the bedside of my lover for the trife side of another

For a cold cell in hell

I abandoned love for the approval of someone else

My soul is on fire

Inside, anxiety is burning me up

But outside the world feels so cold to me

While the flames rip in and out of my chest uncontrollably

I know this ain't the way life is suppose to be

My soul is on fire

My brain bakes in a sweltering inferno of thoughts and memories

While my body is froze in a cryogenic state

There is no crying in hell

Tears just evaporate

My soul is on fire

I'm dying for a breath of fresh air, but it burns to breathe

I'm dying to quench my thirst but water just transmutes to steam

I'm in a state of purgatory where fossils and skeletal remains melt into liquid soil

And oil is in full boil under flames fighting each other over raging seas

My soul is on fire

My dreams are like ceresin

Enraging the blazing inside my chest

I'm terrified to sleep

But lord knows I need the rest

My soul is on fire

The sirens never stop ringing

Gunshots baselines are streaming, under vocal placements of screaming

While Angels are mourning and weeping, the Demons are constantly singing

As flames dance across my chest to these tracks that never stop beating

My soul is on fire

I'm a pressure cooker percolating, pushing out steam

"I did it all for the cream!"

"I kept it real with my team!"

Just a young thug's vision, of living a street dream.

My soul is on fire

Dakota Man! Tell 'em

All the way turned up will get you all the way burnt up

Sitting in a cold cell

Burning in Hell!

My Soul is on fire

I'm burning Alive!

So many fools come and go and never realize

We choose Heaven or Hell by the way we live our lives.

By L. Maurice Martin, A. K. A. "Pain"

Section Nine

Soul collection

"Quotes"
My 7 cents

Quotes

A father's love is the footsteps a daughter follows to find the man of her dreams.

A mother's love is like the coolness in the air that speaks volumes to the soul of her daughters, teaching them to love, learn, teach and help break cycles.

The vibrations of the wind remind me father, that your wisdom is timeless.

The truth about loss is that it is secretly a gift.

Be honest with yourself, for you will never find a better liar.

I have packed all my troubles in my red suit case and I have stored it in my basement which is where I intend to leave it.

A kiss is a picture painted on your lips, not worth a thousand words, but it is a stolen moment in time, with a little truth mixed with a little lie.

Work of the heart has healing properties. These elements touch those you come in contact. Often you may find that in serving others you have mended your own soul and many others along the way.

Life is like a waterfall. You can rush, you can down pour, you can pour, you can be fulfilled or fill others.

Celebrate colored girls because they are triumphant regardless of their rain and rainbows!

We ride on the wings of our brothers and sisters, be thoughtful, be kind and listen to the wind.

Give love, compassion, peace, kindness, empathy and hope. Someone has never received these gifts.

Poverty is not my name, it may be my current circumstance but it does not define my destiny.

Twilight is one step behind me, but it offers promise of a new day and I choose to be great in it.

A dream is a personally created map with a distinct path to your future self.

If you can't be your best, you should work hard until you create what better looks like.

Greatness and purpose is defined by the smallest of dream and fueled by the inner spirit.

Remember life will happen but death should be the only thing that stops you from keeping your dream alive.

My socioeconomic status is not a reflection of my future self. Look upon me with hope, teach me all you can and allow me to grow.

Accept your pain, honor your path then turn that energy into power to fulfill your purpose.

Honor moments with your children and witness the reflections of your life.

Think like a woman and act with love, power and principle.

Daughters should pray as they walk, and the scribe of life will make your path clear.

Ladies remember you are not an amusement park; you can only go for that same old ride, but so many times.

Fight fear and follow your faith, Turn your pain into power to fuel your passions.

Don't stand in the shadows of your dreams watching them fade away.

Love is not 50 50 but it can be a cool 70 30 or a sweet 60 40 but trade it in if it is a sorry 80 20.

Blurred vision on a clear a day makes for exhaustion.

A mother's love never dies; she lives on in your face, lips and thighs.

You have not suffered anything, until you have learned the lesson.

I do not know if my children are geniuses or not, but I am going to give them every opportunity to figure that out for themselves.

If you are trying to accomplish a goal don't allow anyone to get in your way, because that is all some people know how to do, further more they do not know how to get out of their own way.

Everyone makes mistakes, but smart people only make mistakes they can live with.

Patience is a virtue, when the right thing comes along you will appreciate it more and value the journey.

I do not like to shop, but I am just damn good at it.

The truth is the vision that is projected from within and cannot be denied.

Letting go is the ability to see the future without you in it.

Fear is an interrupter of dreams and a barrier to success, but it only stops those who give into the illusion as if it is real.

Each of us can be replaced but none of us can be replicated.

Buckets, don't look in mine, please watch out for your own spills because you're dripping on me.

Never seek advice from the person you have a problem with, they will only tell you how to treat them better.

Afterword

I have a timeless love and it reigns supreme, the love of the life is my lover for life. What about you and your love? Celebrate the one you love today, unashamed and unabashedly, do it because you love to love. Let love in your heart and just smile knowing it is yours to hold for that particular moment. Bask in the glow and warmth from the one you love. Cheers to your love and mine…

Love Always Autumn Reign

Proceeds

1 dollar of each book sale will go to Brotherhood Inc:

Brotherhood Inc. is a 501(c)(3) non-profit organization that seeks to uplift and empower young African American males, ages 16-24, who had involvement with the juvenile or adult criminal justice system, gangs, or who are at risk of such involvement. Brotherhood is a comprehensive reintegration and prevention program that strives to take a holistic approach through comprehensive, culturally-sensitive social services, educational opportunities and on-site employment. Brotherhood, Inc. was developed as a grassroots, community-based response to help break the devastating cycle of poverty, unemployment and incarceration facing young African American males in the twin cities of Minnesota.

Brotherhood Inc
625 University Ave
Suite #203
Saint Paul, MN 55104
651-368-8746
Info@brotherhoodmn.org

Made in the USA
Lexington, KY
16 October 2012